HOW TO SAY NO

100 Quotes To Instil Confidence And Clarity

Om Books International

Om Books International

Reprinted in 2025

Corporate & Editorial Office
A-12, Sector 64, Noida 201 301
Uttar Pradesh, India
Phone: +91 120 477 4100
Email: editorial@ombooks.com
Website: www.ombooksinternational.com

Sales Office
107, Ansari Road, Darya Ganj,
New Delhi 110 002, India
Phone: +91 11 4000 9000
Email: sales@ombooks.com
Website: www.ombooks.com

ISBN: 978-93-63955-09-7

Printed in India

10 9 8 7 6 5 4 3 2

To..

From..

The art of leadership is saying no, not yes. It is very easy to say yes.

Tony Blair

You have to decide what your **highest priorities** are and have the courage pleasantly, smilingly, nonapologetically to say '**no**' to other things. And the way to do that is by having a bigger 'yes' burning inside.

Stephen Covey

Half of the troubles of this life can be traced to saying **yes** too quickly and not saying **no** soon enough.

Josh Billings

**Learn to say
'no' to the good
so you can say
'yes' to the best.**

John C. Maxwell

No

is a complete sentence.

Anne Lamott

The difference between successful people and really successful people is that really successful people say no to almost everything.

Warren Buffett

Saying no can be the ultimate self-care.

Claudia Black

You don't have to accept things you are not okay with.

Anonymous

When you say yes to others, make sure you are not saying no to yourself.

Paulo Coelho

It's only by saying **no** that you can concentrate on the things that are really important.

Steve Jobs

Sometimes you have to say no to others to say **yes to yourself.**

Anonymous

Give yourself the permission to say no without feeling guilty, mean, or selfish.

Anonymous

If you don't
learn to say
no,
you'll
overcommit
every time.

Anonymous

THE ABILITY TO SAY NO IS A TREMENDOUS ADVANTAGE FOR AN INVESTOR.

Warren Buffett

The art of knowing is knowing what to **ignore**.

Rumi

Saying no frees you up to say yes when it matters most.

Adam Grant

Saying no
is not about
rejecting
others,
but about
respecting
yourself.

Anonymous

A '**no**' uttered from the deepest conviction is better than a '**yes**' merely uttered to please, or worse, to avoid trouble.

Mahatma Gandhi

The oldest, shortest words— 'yes' and 'no'— are those which require the most thought.

Pythagoras

Sometimes, no is the kindest word.

Vironika Tugaleva

SAY NO TO
EVERYTHING,
SO YOU CAN
SAY YES TO
THE ONE THING.

Richie Norton

Say no, then negotiate.

Anonymous

A no to
one thing
is a yes to
another.

Anonymous

Learn to say no to the demands of the world. Say yes to the longings of your own heart.

Jonathan Lockwood Huie

Say no to anything that doesn't bring you peace.

Anonymous

Say no to distraction, so you can say yes to your destiny.

Anonymous

SAY NO WITHOUT FEELING GUILTY.

Anonymous

BE BRAVE ENOUGH TO SAY NO WHEN IT'S EASIER TO SAY YES.

Anonymous

Don't say
maybe
if you want to
say no.

Paulo Coelho

You have to learn to say no without feeling guilty.

Anonymous

The ability to say no is an essential ingredient in a happy life.

Anonymous

The art of saying no involves knowing when to say it and how to say it.

Anonymous

YOU CAN'T
SAY YES TO
EVERYTHING
AND EXPECT
TO HAVE TIME
FOR THE
THINGS THAT
MATTER MOST.

Anonymous

Saying no can be liberating and empowering.

Anonymous

YOU CAN
SAY NO WITH
KINDNESS
AND
RESPECT.

Anonymous

Saying no is a way to **protect your boundaries.**

Anonymous

WHEN YOU SAY NO TO THE WRONG THINGS, YOU MAKE ROOM TO SAY YES TO THE RIGHT THINGS.

Anonymous

Saying no allows you to be more present and engaged with the things you say yes to.

Anonymous

SAYING NO IS NOT ABOUT REJECTION; IT'S ABOUT **PRIORITIZATION**.

Anonymous

Learn to say no without explaining yourself.

Anonymous

Saying no can be an act of **self-love** and self-respect.

Anonymous

Saying no means you value your time and energy.

Anonymous

YOU HAVE THE RIGHT TO SAY NO WITHOUT FEELING GUILTY.

Anonymous

Saying no is a skill that can be developed and refined.

Anonymous

NO IS A POWERFUL WORD WHEN USED WITH INTENTION.

Anonymous

Saying no can be a form of self-care.

Anonymous

A WELL-TIMED NO CAN SAVE YOU FROM UNNECESSARY STRESS.

Anonymous

Saying no can help you maintain your focus and productivity.

Anonymous

You can say no and still be a kind and compassionate person.

Anonymous

Saying no
can help
you maintain
your personal
boundaries and
integrity.

Anonymous

Saying no is not about being selfish; it's about being self-aware.

Anonymous

No is a complete sentence that doesn't require justification.

Anonymous

YOU HAVE TO
HAVE A LIFE.
YOU HAVE TO
SAY

NO.

Howard Behar

SAYING NO CAN CREATE SPACE FOR MORE MEANINGFUL AND FULFILLING EXPERIENCES.

Anonymous

Saying no is a way to honor your own needs and desires.

Anonymous

Saying no
can help
you avoid
burnout and
exhaustion.

Anonymous

SAYING NO CAN HELP YOU MAINTAIN BALANCE AND HARMONY IN YOUR LIFE.

Anonymous

Saying no is a way to take control of your own life.

Anonymous

You have the power to say no to anything that doesn't serve you.

Anonymous

SAYING NO CAN BE A FORM OF SELF-EMPOWERMENT.

Anonymous

Saying no can be the ultimate self-care.

Marie Forleo

THE ART OF SAYING NO IS REALLY THE ART OF CHOOSING.

Anonymous

SAYING NO CAN HELP YOU CREATE A LIFE THAT IS ALIGNED WITH YOUR VALUES AND PASSIONS.

Anonymous

SAYING NO CAN HELP YOU STAY TRUE TO YOURSELF.

Anonymous

You can say no
with respect,
you can say no
with dignity,
and you can
say no with
kindness.

Seth Godin

Self-care
has a higher
priority than
giving care.

Damon Zahariades

A great piece of advice: say no to almost everything.

Jim Collins

Learn to say no. Don't let your mouth overload your back.

Jim Rohn

SAYING NO IS NOT A REJECTION, IT'S A REDIRECTION.

Anonymous

Saying no is not about being selfish, it's about being true to yourself.

Anonymous

A 'NO' DOES NOT MEAN YOU ARE REJECTING THE PERSON. IT MEANS YOU ARE REJECTING THE REQUEST.

Amit Kalantri

The most successful people are not those who have the most talent or work the hardest, but rather those who say no the most often.

Mark Manson

SAYING NO CAN HELP YOU CREATE MORE SPACE FOR THE THINGS THAT TRULY MATTER TO YOU.

Anonymous

Saying no can help you stay focused on your goals and dreams.

Anonymous

Saying no can
help you protect
your time and
energy for the
things that
bring you joy.

Anonymous

Saying no can help you avoid unnecessary obligations and commitments.

Anonymous

Saying no to others is saying yes to yourself.

Anonymous

Saying no is a sign of respect.

Anonymous

Saying no can be liberating.

Anonymous

Saying no can help you create more space for the things that make you happy.

Anonymous

SAYING NO CAN HELP YOU STAY TRUE TO YOUR VALUES AND PRIORITIES.

Anonymous

Saying no can help you avoid unnecessary stress.

Anonymous

SAYING NO CAN HELP YOU MAINTAIN A HEALTHY WORK-LIFE BALANCE.

Anonymous

Saying no can help you protect your time and energy for the things that matter most.

Anonymous

Saying no can help you create a life that is more aligned with your values and passions.

Anonymous

Saying no can help you avoid feeling overwhelmed and overcommitted.

Anonymous

Saying no can help you stay focused on your goals and aspirations.

Anonymous

Saying no can help you maintain your mental and emotional well-being.

Anonymous

Saying no can help you create more space for joy and fulfillment in your life.

Anonymous

Saying no can help you avoid unnecessary stress and anxiety.

Anonymous

Saying no
can help you
stay focused
on your
priorities and
commitments.

Anonymous

Saying no
can help you
maintain your
sense of self
and identity.

Anonymous

Saying no can help you create a life that is more **balanced** and **fulfilling**.

Anonymous

Saying no can help you maintain healthy relationships and boundaries.

Anonymous

Saying no
can help you
avoid feeling
resentful and
burnt out.

Anonymous

Saying no can help you create more space for self-care and self-love.

Anonymous

Saying no can help you maintain your sense of peace and tranquility.

Anonymous

Learning to say no is an important skill.

Anonymous

Sometimes saying no is the best form of self-respect.

Anonymous

Focus is
about
saying
no.

Steve Jobs